Gentlemen of Fortune Academia

8 Principles to Get and Keep Your Sh*t Together

Acknowledgements:

I am grateful for all my friends and colleagues encouraging me to start the work, persevere through it, and finally publish it. A special thank you to my beautiful children and extended family. I could have not done it without you. Finally, I would like to acknowledge with gratitude the support and love of my Wife and Aunt Elizabeth.
I love you all.

Table of Contents:

Introduction

Chapter 1: Winners and Losers

Chapter 2: Perception Shapes Reality

Chapter 3: The Power of Self-Reliance

Chapter 4: The Influence of Articulation

Chapter 5: Belief

Chapter 6: Creating Opportune Moments

Chapter 7: Love and Gratitude

Chapter 8: Action

Conclusion

Bonus Chapter

Introduction:

This book is not just a compilation of words; it's a journey through the corridors of my life, a narrative spun from victories and defeats, and a collection of invaluable lessons gleaned from both the living and those who've left an indelible mark on this world.

As I reflect on the moments shared with both loved ones and passing strangers, I find the rich tapestry of experiences has woven the fabric of this self-help guide.

In every chapter, you'll discover attitudes and decisions that stem directly from the crucible of lessons learned. Some were hard-fought battles, each incident serving as a poignant brushstroke on the canvas of my life, solidifying the authenticity of the principles presented in these pages.

I hold a firm belief that within each of us resides a superhero, endowed with extraordinary strengths and abilities. This book is a testament to the untapped potential that lies within you. Drawing on my own experiences, I recognize that talent is abundant in this world, yet the challenge lies in transforming these talents into a force that reshapes the corporate landscape. It's about turning Superman into Clark Kent, about being a powerful superhero capable of soaring through the world and even reversing time—while donning a suit, navigating the workplace, and perhaps reading this book in the breakroom. So, let's embark on a transformative journey together. Let's channel your superpowers and abilities towards the dynamic arena of the business world. In the following chapters, we'll unravel the secrets to unleashing your potential and navigating the complexities of life with the finesse of a true superhero in everyday settings. Get ready to embrace your inner Clark Kent and let your extraordinary abilities shine in the world of business and beyond. The adventure begins now.

Chapter 1:

Winners and Losers

Success in life often hinges on the delicate balance between the determination to win and the acceptance that failure is an inevitable part of the journey. As I've always said, "Winners don't always win, but losers never win." This wisdom underscores the importance of resilience and perseverance. In the pursuit of personal and professional goals, one must recognize that setbacks are not indicators of ultimate failure but rather steppingstones toward success. Embracing this mindset sets the stage for a resilient and forward-thinking approach to life's challenges.

2.0 Attitude and Effort, Get 2.0 Results

The correlation between attitude, effort, and results is a fundamental principle that governs the trajectory of personal and professional development. Cultivating a 2.0 attitude involves procrastination and a promise to work harder later, even in the face of adversity. Combine this attitude with intentional and consistent effort not to practice, train or in any way progress, and you'll find yourself achieving 2.0 results. It's merely about doing the bare minimum, but rather about investing the extra effort required to elevate your performance and outcomes. By adopting this philosophy, you stonewall any sense of accomplishment and success in your endeavors. So, please beware. Raw talent can only get you so far. We're all good and we will all be good but how many of us will be great? How many of us will achieve greatness? Let's be great.

The Plague Mindset

One of the most insidious mental barriers to personal growth is the pervasive "Not Enough to

Go Around" mindset. This limiting belief suggests scarcity in opportunities, resources, and success, fostering a sense of competition and fear of lack. This mindset multiplies fear and in turn, breeds desperation. So beware my Gentlemen, some people will begin to prey on others. Be vigilant. Overcoming this mindset involves recognizing the abundance that exists in the world and understanding that success is not a zero-sum game. Shifting towards an abundance mindset opens doors to collaboration, creativity, and a wealth of possibilities that can lead to personal and professional prosperity. All the money is out there, all the success, go seize it.

Winners Have Grit

Grit, the unwavering perseverance, and passion for long-term goals, is a defining trait of winners. In the face of challenges and obstacles, winners display resilience and commitment, refusing to be deterred by temporary setbacks. Cultivating grit involves developing a mindset that views difficulties not as roadblocks but as opportunities for growth. By embracing challenges with determination and maintaining a steadfast focus on long-term objectives, individuals can develop the resilience necessary to navigate the complexities of life and emerge victorious.

Belief Is the Gun, Knowledge Is the Bullet, and Action Is Pulling the Trigger. The metaphorical interplay between belief, knowledge, and action encapsulates the essence of achieving one's goals. Belief serves as the foundation, the metaphorical gun that holds the potential for success. Knowledge acts as the ammunition, providing the necessary insights and skills to propel you forward. However, it is the intentional and strategic action that pulls the trigger, unleashing the full potential of belief and knowledge. Understanding this symbiotic relationship empowers individuals to align their convictions, acquire the requisite knowledge, and take purposeful action, thereby propelling themselves toward success. Winners say," We learn from pain, we are forged in it." It's remarkable to see what people have achieved in life but to know what they have overcome… priceless. Choose to be a winner and go win!

Chapter 2:

Perception Shapes Reality

In the realm of professionalism, the manner in which you present yourself becomes a powerful determinant of how you are perceived and received. Consider your appearance and demeanor as strategic tools in navigating the societal landscape. In essence, treat your attire as a form of disguise; a means to play the game in order to secure your place within it. Recognize the undeniable influence of societal norms and expectations, look good damn it! Although one should not be constrained by them, leveraging this awareness can be especially advantageous. The power of decision lies in your hands— I say choose to embody the success you aspire to achieve. Taking immediate action, such as delving into relevant literature, is a very commendable starting point. Yet, the true essence lies in more than just looking the part; it's about embodying and understanding the role you wish to play, fully. A personal anecdote underscores the significance of this principle. The transformative impact of donning professional attire, eliciting respectful acknowledgments, compared to the more casual days, serves as a testament to the influence of appearance. Strive to maintain this focus, especially during pivotal moments like interviews or client meetings. This is your life, and the world is your stage, take pride in your appearance. It's been said," Dressing nice is a form of good manners and dressing appropriately for the occasion, makes you a Gentleman." Key attributes to cultivate include a commanding posture, unwavering confidence, a firm handshake, and maintaining direct eye contact.

These elements collectively project an image of authority and competence. It is crucial to internalize the notion that you are a leader—now, act accordingly. However, this is a double-edged sword Gentlemen. Safeguard your reputation by embodying strong values and morals. Your external image should authentically reflect the principles you truly hold. In this pursuit, avoid any unnecessary embellishments; let your authenticity shine through. Practical tips to enhance your professional image include mastering the art of tying a tie and understanding your preferred suit tailoring. If a bespoke suit is beyond your current financial reach, opt for off-the-rack options that closely align with your body type. Consider this initial investment as a long-term commitment—a timeless ensemble waiting in your closet, poised to enhance your appearance whenever the need arises.

Consider the following highlights from this chapter.

Strategic Disguise:

Treat your clothing as a disguise to navigate societal expectations. Dress for the occasion intentionally.

Decisive Power: Your decision to embody success is the first step toward achieving it. Choose to be the new you and stick to it.

Beyond Appearance: Acting the part is valuable, but understanding and internalizing your role is paramount. Know your business.

Powerful Presence: Command attention with a confident posture, firm handshake, and direct eye contact.

Authenticity Matters: Safeguard your reputation by authentically embodying your values and morals. Be memorable but never make a scene.

Practical Tips: Learn practical skills like tying a tie and understanding suit tailoring to enhance your professional image. Classic vs new. Go classic.

Long-Term Investment: Even on a budget, invest in off-the-rack options that align with your body type for lasting impact.

Chapter 3:

The Power of Self-Reliance

In the journey toward getting and keeping your sh*t in order, a fundamental truth must be acknowledged: No One is Coming to Save You. This realization is pivotal for success, as life demands a profound sense of self and self-reliance. Society often perpetuates the narrative that the good guy always triumphs in the end, but this, I believe, is one of the greatest falsehoods we've been fed. Contrary to the notion of staying under the radar, success demands boldness. It necessitates standing up, claiming what you deserve, and demonstrating strength and competence. Comparably close to a cold breeze walking in the room, this is the goal. To ascend in any field, you must embody the qualities of a leader. Doing so not only propels you forward but also acts as a deterrent to those with ill intentions. In my experience, malevolent individuals target the vulnerable. Much like predators targeting the weak animals at the rear of the herd, your responsibility is to move to the front and assert yourself. Playing the victim only invites trouble.

Embrace solitude without fear. There is a difference between being alone and feeling lonely. Learn and know the difference.

Accountability is the key to freedom. Understand that persistence is a conscious choice, much like any other decision in life. This is your journey and you choosing to be a better you, is the best gift you can ever give for yourself. Be excited, it's ok. The flame within you must burn hotter than the water thrown on it. While people may wish you well to your face, it's crucial to recognize that they may not want you to ever surpass them.

Trusting that others will always act in their self-interest is a prudent mindset. While enemies are always predictable in their animosity, friends may not always stand by you, especially if defending you carries negative consequences for them. Don't cry about it.

Instead of asking for an easier path, strive to become better. Life, after all, is a do-it-yourself project. Take control of your desires, keeping them few and formulating a plan to achieve them. Then desire more and repeat. With a superhuman level of perspicacity, anticipating all aspects of life is essential. Mental traps abound, with the past and the future being the most daunting walls. Resist the allure of the past's seemingly safe door, for it may hold pain and stagnation. As for the future, with its blinding lights and infinite possibilities, it might be intimidating. Yet, it is the very gateway to the life you desire. Many find themselves in a mental waiting room, hesitating, but it's crucial to understand that No One is Coming to Save You, EVER. Remember, you can be the brightest, shiniest, most appealing lightbulb and there still will be people always that prefer the dark. The power to shape your destiny lies within you.

Let's delve into the key highlights:

No one is coming to save you:

Life demands a profound sense of self and self-reliance for success. Look within, not out. Challenge the notion that the good guy always wins; doing the right thing doesn't always attract attention and your movement needs attention.

Boldness, strength, and competence are essential for personal advancement.

Demonstrate Leadership:

Act confidently and assertively to rise through the ranks professionally and personally. Displaying qualities of leadership helps deter negative influences.

Be Wary of Weakness:

Bad people often target the vulnerable; assertiveness helps keep them at bay. I'd rather be difficult to deal with then easy to play. Playing the victim makes you susceptible to exploitation, professionally and personally.

Embrace Solitude:

Don't fear being alone; accountability is liberating. Scrape off the dead weight, even if it hurts. They may be not able to go where you're going. Independence is a key element of personal growth.

Choose Persistence: Persistence is a deliberate choice; commitment leads to progress. Find strength in your purpose and keep your foot on the gas.

Navigate Interpersonal Dynamics:

Recognize that people often prioritize their personal interests. Seriously, beware. Trust is delicate; even friends may not always stand by you when it conflicts with their interests.

Seek Improvement, Not Easy Paths: Instead of seeking an easier life, strive to become better. Embrace life as a do-it-yourself project; take charge of your own journey.

Control Desires and Practice Gratitude:

Manage desires; focus on a few attainable goals. Attain and then aim higher. Gratitude helps break mental walls and fosters a positive mindset.

Confront the Doors of the Past and Future:

Resist dwelling on the past; it may seem safe but can hinder progress. The future is full of possibilities; view it as a chance to create the life you desire. Break free from the mental waiting room and take charge.

Key Message:

Life is a journey of self-reliance and personal responsibility. Embrace boldness, demonstrate real leadership, and fiercely persist in the face of challenges. Navigate interpersonal dynamics with awareness and seek improvement, not an easy way out. Remember, No One is Coming to Save You—be your own Hero.

Chapter 4:

The Influence of Articulation

In the pursuit of maintaining equilibrium in one's life, an often underestimated yet powerful tool is the skillful use of language. The impact of words extends beyond mere communication—they possess the ability to trigger biochemical reactions, including the release of serotonin and endorphins. Within this paradigm, I advocate for a theory that posits the existence of an optimal response or phraseology in any given situation, capable of eliciting desired outcomes through the orchestration of chemical reactions in one's favor. "The Phrase That Pays," either financially or receiving the desired outcome. The essence of words lies in their intrinsic power and tangible energy. It is imperative to understand that the energy emitted by our words necessitates reciprocity; thus, maintaining an aura of love and positivity is fundamental. Attempting to diminish others only serves to disrupt this delicate equilibrium, manifesting a palpable dissonance in the energy exchange. The English language, with its inherent beauty, provides a vast canvas for expression. Mastery of language allows for the incorporation of charm and an expanded vocabulary, adding layers to interpersonal interactions. Trust, a cornerstone in relationships—whether with clients, colleagues, or friends—constitutes an indispensable element for success. Upholding one's word holds profound influence, as it shapes not only your personal world but the world at large. Speaking things into existence contributes to the development of a powerful consistency, a trait synonymous with enduring success.

However, with great power comes responsibility. As you cultivate your prowess in spoken communication, it is essential to remain vigilant against the allure of manipulation. Succumbing to this temptation can lead down a dark path devoid of true joy and success, as these qualities cannot be authentically achieved through deceit or harm. A poignant reminder is extended, emphasizing that proficiency in any skill should not be employed to inflict harm upon others. It's not becoming of a Gentlemen. Whether in the realm of salesmanship, interpersonal relationships, or personal endeavors, leveraging your newfound ability should focus on efficient and compassionate self-expression, rather than manipulation. Through the mastery of the spoken word, one attains genuine power and self-control. Standing by one's word, delivering promises with unwavering commitment, and taking ownership of mistakes contribute to the establishment of a formidable character. Embracing brief moments of discomfort is a requisite for growth. Concluding debates with humility, admitting when wrong, and vowing improvement showcase a profound strength. Refraining from engaging in futile blame-casting and excusing irrational behavior distinguishes the mature individual from the rest, positioning their mindset and emotions above the chaos. The realization of your communicative power is most evident when you speak your truth. However, wisdom lies in recognizing when silence is the most eloquent response. A strategic absence of words invites introspection considering who speaks, why, and discerning the meaningful from the inconsequential.

A cardinal rule emerges: "Never argue with a fool, because people at a distance you can't tell who is who." Choosing composure, logic, and the mature act of agreeing to disagree further elevate one above petty conflict. Words have historically inspired nations and foster teamwork. The grandeur of a stadium's 40,000 fans synchronized in the "wave" exemplifies the beauty achievable through collaborative effort. It's Beautiful.

Harness the true power within your words,

deploying them judiciously. Disclosing just enough about yourself fosters an air of mystery and curiosity. Over sharing or embellishing tend to have a negative effect, resulting in people not believing you or simply tuning you out. The more you know early on, the less you want to know later. Stay mysterious. In interactions, exhibit genuine interest in others by asking questions and expressing gratitude for shared insights. Confidence in navigating awkward moments adds a layer of strength to your character. When you speak, be specific to eliminate ambiguity. Always maintain politeness, coupled with boldness—an amalgamation that exudes confidence and assertiveness. In a world thirsting for love, be the catalyst for change by spreading words of kindness, understanding, and appreciation. Remember, being genuinely interested in others sets you apart from the indifferent crowd. Confidently express your anticipation for future conversations, and let your words be a source of positivity and encouragement in a world that so often craves it.

Chapter 5:

Belief

"Embrace the notion that life unfolds with purpose, amor fati"

In this pivotal chapter, we explore the profound impact of belief on our journey to getting and keeping our sh*t together. Life is hard and leading a successful life is no less difficult. We are the amalgamation of our experiences, both adverse and advantageous, whether by our choices or by fate. Belief is immensely difficult and will give you far more difficulties to practice than any other chapter. Remember faith is life's most beautiful poetry. The foundation of strength lies in acknowledging that we possess inherent power, capable of achieving extraordinary feats.

THE ESSENCE OF SUCCESS AND FULFILLMENT ORIGINATES INTERNALLY

Would you ever attempt to wield your special abilities if you were unaware of their existence? Like to fly for example. It's doubtful. We are inherently designed for greatness, and the knowledge to amplify our capabilities are readily accessible in this modern age. Everything you need is at your fingertips. Empower yourself through education and guard the flame of your potential fiercely. Nurture the subtle burn that generates authentic energy, fueling your belief. Believe in your dream and you will begin to move, and the universe will start to move with you. Mental well-being, an extensively explored topic in numerous books, is undeniably crucial. Maintaining a tranquil and focused mind is imperative to sustain your connection to self-belief. While meditation is a valuable tool, persist in embracing your beliefs and maintaining positivity, even to the point of unwavering conviction. Live your truth, acting in accordance with your beliefs. Those who have succeeded may not reveal their secrets—forge your own path and trust that success is on its way. We gravitate towards the familiar, if fear and doubt persist, they become the constants in your life. Your mind functions as a magnet, and the fruits of your efforts may not materialize immediately. Play the long game, preparing for inevitable challenges. Recognize that rainy days nurture the seeds of growth. Don't let envy and hatred blind you to the potential lessons that others can impart.

SETTING YOUR GOALS HIGH CAN MAKE YOUR FAILURES SURPASS OTHERS' ACHIEVEMENTS

Have faith in the process and practice patience. Consider you went back in time and found a young actor still searching for their breakthrough role and having a hard time. If given the chance to speak to a young, talented actor down and out, you'd encourage perseverance, assuring them that greatness awaits. You're going to be huge star! Trust in the journey, and remember, achieving personal excellence surpasses the quest to outshine others. There's no nobility in outperforming your peers; surpassing your former self is a far more worthy endeavor.

Cultivate an unwavering positive outlook, not merely hoping for a favorable outcome, but maintaining a resolute energy until your goals are realized. Imagine the boundless dreams you'd pursue if failure were not a possibility—tap into that empowering sensation.

TO ALTER YOUR NARRATIVE, TRANSFORM YOUR INNER DIALOGUE

Your inner monologue may be the anchor holding you back. Recognize that this voice is malleable, capable of being reshaped. How can you achieve greatness when your own thoughts declare it impossible? Begin there. Some closures in life may never materialize; accept this and move forward. When your tumultuous past attempts to resurface, shut it out. Embrace the reality that certain things can never return to the way they once was. Unshakeable belief in yourself renders you unstoppable. When your past calls, redirect those thoughts to voicemail, forging ahead.

Remember………

IF YOU ALLOW GRIEF TO TRANSFORM INTO ANGER, IT PERSISTS. YOUR DRIVE MUST OVERPOWER YOUR FEARS

Let's delve into the key highlights:

Empowering Beliefs:

Embrace the understanding that we are the product of our experiences, whether chosen or not. Maintain the empowering belief that you are powerful and capable of achieving great things.

Internal Success and Achievement:

Recognize that the feeling of success and achievement originates from within. Unleash your inner potential by acknowledging your inherent abilities and seeking knowledge readily available in the digital age.

Protecting Your Energy:

Acknowledge the realness of energy and the importance of safeguarding your inner flame. Cultivate a quiet burn that fuels genuine belief.

Prioritize mental health through practices like meditation, ensuring a quiet and focused mind to preserve your connection to your goals.

Long-Term Vision:

Understand the magnetism of the mind and the tendency to attract what is familiar. Plan for the long game, anticipating challenges and using them as opportunities for growth. Remember, it's the rainy days that water the seeds of success.

Ambitious Goals and Failures:

Set your goals high, understanding that your failures at this elevated level may surpass the successes of others. Trust the process, be patient, and draw inspiration from the journeys of those who faced initial challenges before achieving greatness.

Positive Outlook and Self-Improvement:

Cultivate an unyielding positive outlook on life. Strive not just to be better than others but to surpass your former self continually. Dream without fear of failure, realizing the power of self-belief even in the face of uncertainty.

Changing Your Inner Monologue:

Acknowledge and transform your inner monologue. Challenge and change the voice in your head that may be holding you back. Accept that closure may not always come, but you have the power to move forward, embracing new beginnings without being shackled by the past.

Motivation Overcoming Fear:

Understand the transformative power of motivation, surpassing the grip of fear. Face grief without letting it morph into perpetual anger. Recognize that true motivation is the force that propels you beyond your fears, enabling you to conquer challenges. By internalizing and applying these principles, you are poised to strengthen your belief system and navigate the path towards a more fulfilling and purposeful life. Remember, your journey is uniquely yours, and by embracing these principles, you empower yourself to shape your narrative and overcome obstacles with resilience and grace.

Chapter 6:

Creating Opportune Moments

In the pursuit of success, many attribute a significant part of their journey to luck. However, luck, in my perspective, is not merely a happenstance event; it can be cultivated through deliberate actions and a focused mindset. Yes! An often-deemed elusive force can be harnessed. How do you, positively create luck? That I do not actually know but I do know you must be worthy of lucks touch.

This chapter explores the concept of luck,

emphasizing the importance of preparation and seizing opportunities.

Strategic Effort and Readiness

Luck, I believe, is not a random occurrence but a result of working diligently toward a goal and being prepared for unforeseen opportunities. A key attribute to attaining it is maintaining focus on your craft and continuously striving for self-improvement. Picture yourself in a room or a situation where achieving your goal seems effortless – that, I contend, is the manifestation of strategic effort and readiness. Conversely, lack of preparation can turn a seemingly fortunate situation into a stroke of bad luck. It has various forms, surrounds us, and being receptive to it requires both awareness and active engagement. However, true luck is only realized when you seize the opportunity with preparedness and action.

The Power of Energy and Passion

Creating your own luck involves more than mere chance, it also requires investing time and effort in cultivating habits and ideas discussed in previous chapters as well. Your passion and belief in your own success emit an energy that draws people towards you. This energy becomes a magnet, attracting individuals who want to support and assist you in your endeavors. The question shifts from "if" to "when" you will achieve success, fueled by the energy that others sense in you. When we're called upon to use our real passions and abilities, that energy will always be easy to locate. This magnetic energy, what we often term as "luck," is a result of your dedication and hard work. It positions you to capitalize on opportunities when they arise. However, luck, no matter how abundant, is futile without preparation. Meeting a potential benefactor or collaborator will be of little consequence if you present yourself as disheveled or unprepared.

A Choice of Resilience

Mistakes and missed opportunities are part of the journey. In the face of setbacks, you have a choice—let them be a source of despair or view them as valuable lessons. A resilient mindset, coupled with the principles that have been outlined, ensures that setbacks become steppingstones to future success.

Embracing Future Opportunities

By implementing the beliefs and strategies discussed in this chapter, you pave the way for luck to strike again. The next time an opportunity arises, you'll be not only ready but deserving of the support and connections that may come your way.

In summary, luck is not merely a roll of the dice; it's a force that can be harnessed through preparation, positive energy, and a strategic mindset.

The principles outlined here provide a roadmap

for creating and maximizing the luck you need to

propel yourself towards success.

Chapter 7:

Love and Gratitude

In this chapter, we delve into the transformative power of love and gratitude. As the saying goes, "Please and Thank you, these are the magic words," and indeed, they are the keys to unlocking meaningful connections and personal growth. It's not just always about who you are but who are you becoming? Love and kindness are the language the whole world understands, get familiar and be well versed. Kindness is free, pass it around.

Cultivating Genuine Connections

To win with people, take a sincere interest in them. Engage in genuine conversations by actively listening and asking questions. Providing others with a platform to share their thoughts and experiences not only separates you from the crowd but also builds meaningful relationships. Leading from the front, daring to care, and surrounding yourself with the right people are crucial steps in the journey to success.

The Infectious Power of Gratitude

Have you encountered individuals radiating

gratitude for the good things in their lives? Their positive energy is infectious. By focusing on gratitude, you tap into a powerful force that fills your optimism tank. Much like the Care Bears spreading warmth with their feelings of love, beaming out of their chest, your positivity can light up the world. Gratitude with precise use of the magic words, can move mountains.

Living by Love and Gratitude

Imagine living by the words "love and gratitude." What benefits could this mindset bring to your life? Rather than dwelling on potential harm, consider the positive impacts. Embracing these principles diminishes ego and selfishness, creating space for a life of purpose and service.

Rising from Challenges

Life may not always be smooth, and hitting rock bottom is far from pleasant. I know. However, find joy in the possibilities that emerge from challenges. Even in moments of despair, express gratitude for the opportunity to fight another day. Reflect on personal setbacks as opportunities for growth and resilience.

Empowerment Through Service

Empowered people empower others. Share your passion and resist the temptation to conform to perceived norms of success. Hard work and focus, not secret sauces, lead to success. Be known for your generosity and kindness, and ask yourself, "What am I doing for others?" True love is revealed through shared joys and sorrows, not just in words but in deeds.

The Power of Being in Service

Being in service to others is not just an obligation; it's an opportunity to use your talents for the greater good. Rise to the challenge, make eye contact, and commit to delivering on your promises. Being of service provides a chance to align your actions with your true self, finding joy in activities that resonate with your interests.

Acceptance and True Freedom

Knowing oneself is not enough; it's about accepting your true self. This acceptance marks a groundbreaking shift, offering the ultimate freedom to be your authentic self without apology. When you want for nothing, you already possess everything.

In conclusion, living a life guided by love and

gratitude is a journey toward fulfillment and purpose. Embrace these principles and watch as your life transforms into a beacon of positivity, impacting not only yourself but those around you.

Chapter 8:

Action

In the realm of personal development, action is the cornerstone that transforms aspirations into reality. It's the force behind the scenes, the silent hero celebrated behind closed doors. Without action, there is no propulsion toward our goals. To manifest your ambitions, you must possess the tenacity to act and the integrity to do the work. Cutting corners may seem tempting, but lasting success demands adherence to the right path. Success, without exception, comes at a cost. Being a person of action implies embracing substance and paying the full price, ethically and diligently. Trust, a crucial currency in any endeavor, is earned by fostering confidence through impeccable character. To navigate the journey toward your goals, you need reliable connections. Strive to be recognized as an individual with high standards and unwavering ethics. This might seem like a tall order, but achieving your aspirations necessitates such pillars to guide your path. I want you not just to exist but to truly live until the end. Living in the present is paramount; it is the crucible from which genuine action emerges. While you may lack immediate resources or connections, initiating action will attract them. Hard work is non-negotiable; excuses have no place in the pursuit of your goals. However, remember that not every moment requires external action. Allow yourself time for introspection, rest, and proper sleep, as moments of silence and contemplation often lead to clarity. In popular culture, we often celebrate the end product, the alpha dog, or the hero, but the relentless hard work behind the scenes are frequently overlooked. Watching someone study or practice for an entire episode might not be entertaining, of your favorite drama and that's why the montage or fast forwarded. But it is the unwavering commitment to action that propels them forward. Action is not an isolated event; it is a continuous, unyielding force. "You don't know what you don't know." Oh, I like that one. Acquiring new knowledge, ideas, and perspectives is vital for personal growth, but it requires deliberate effort. My life changed when I took the initiative to read independently. The catalyst was a simple internet search for the "Top 10 self-help Books," leading to a transformative journey. However, reading alone is insufficient; the real change occurs when you apply what you've learned. I read for years without any impact until the day I acted. It's a daily grind, requiring hourly dedication to implementing new habits and approaches. Your fairytale is worth fighting for, and procrastination may inadvertently hand your opportunities to others. Building a life of happiness and fulfillment is a form of self-care. In a world that often advises caution and safety, pursuing anything worthwhile demands 100% focus and burning passion. Losers make backup plans; champions commit fully and endure suffering and pain to achieve extraordinary feats. Not all money is good money; beware of deceptive opportunities that seem too good to be true. Sharpen your mind, body, and actions to discern genuine prospects from potential pitfalls. Think of it as building a house—simple in concept but never easy or quick. Patience is crucial as you refine your skills and vigilance against stagnation.

Experience is the best teacher, as real-life situations on a grand stage shape your perceptions and beliefs. Seek out new experiences eagerly, whether through travel, literature, or volunteering, as they contribute significantly to personal growth. The equation for risk is probability multiplied by severity, and trust is the antidote to the feeling of risk. Trust in yourself and in the processes, you've established to achieve your goals. Understanding the importance of each component is essential; mere motion without comprehension is futile.

Working towards personal success demands time and devotion, often accompanied by feelings of guilt and perceived selfishness. Embrace the grind, as it is through action that mental toughness is cultivated. When motivation wanes, discipline becomes the anchor, and discipline is a byproduct of consistent action. Your meticulous attention to detail might stem from a fear of making mistakes, hindering progress. Acknowledge that perfection was discovered through imperfection, and success most often requires embracing risks and sacrifices. If you were given the opportunity to build your dream home, for free? Yes, for free. But the catch is you must build it yourself….

Would you rise to the occasion, educate yourself, and put in the effort for the most significant investment of your life? Be honest….

People may come and go swiftly in life, and if your absence doesn't faze them, your presence might not have meant anything. Keep acting, keep moving forward, for in sustained action lies the path to your aspirations. Lights, camera, its

ACTION TIME!

Conclusion:

In conclusion, I firmly believe that each principle discussed in this book holds indispensable value. It is not a matter of suggesting that these principles operate independently of one another; rather, there exists a profound harmony when they are integrated into the fabric of a marriage. These principles, when embraced, have the power to transform not only your approach to life but also the dynamics of your relationships. As you embark on your journey, take these principles, and weave them into the very essence of your being. Ground yourself firmly, pressing your feet to the earth, as you propel towards success. Be bold in your endeavors, yet let politeness and professionalism guide your actions. Approach your plans and actions with unwavering determination, yet always maintain a sense of respect for others. When faced with challenges that demand decisive action, do so with grace and class. Keep a stoic mindset, mastering the art of keeping your emotions in check, allowing resilience and determination to guide you through both triumphs and tribulations. Strive for success not only through achievement but also by embodying the qualities of a true gentleman—upholding good values and maintaining a sense of refinement. In essence, this journey is about winning through resilience and embracing the pains of growth. Picture yourself in a sharp suit throughout this transformative process, symbolizing the elegance and poise that accompany success achieved through integrity and principled living. May you find triumph in embodying these principles and, in doing so, create a life marked by both accomplishment and character. Now, go take

over your world.

Bonus Chapter:

Love or Be Loved

With an intriguing question like "Love or Be Loved," the chapter delves into the profound aspects of human connection. Let's explore the dichotomy and what it reveals about our inner selves.

To Love: The Positive

These individuals epitomize optimism, always viewing the glass as half full. They initiate affection, revel in life's pleasures, and passionately engage with people and experiences. By putting others first, they perceive goodness in people, even when individuals struggle to see it in themselves.

The Challenge

Yet, there's a vulnerability in loving deeply; many may not reciprocate. In a world where kindness can be misconstrued as weakness, lovers face potential heartache and disappointment. Despite these challenges, choosing to love can be a transformative journey.

To Be Loved: The Positive

This group often embodies independence focusing on external aspects, such as material success, to attract affection. They maintain a detached demeanor, seemingly indifferent to emotional dependency. Their love is measured and cautious, mirroring what they perceive to have received.

The Struggle

While being loved brings admirers and accolades, there's a persistent feeling of loneliness. Despite external success, the authentic connection may be elusive. The struggle lies in wondering if they are loved for who they truly are or merely for their accomplishments.

The Decision

I reflect on this choice, advocating for love despite potential heartaches. Enduring life's challenges become a learning experience, a process of navigating the waves of lies and misplaced trust. Choosing love fosters meaningful relationships and a deeper connection with the blessing's life offers.

Finding Purpose in Love

Drawing a parallel with the fleeting adoration of

celebrity experiences, I emphasize the desire for genuine, passionate connections. Choosing love, whether for a partner or life itself, provides purpose, grounding us in meaningful actions that lead to prosperity.

Final Thoughts

In the pursuit of purpose and joy, the chapter encourages readers to choose love, recognizing its power to transform and uplift. It urges us to fight for purpose, embracing the profound joy that hides within it.

About the Author:

Jon Green

Keynote Speaker/ Motivational Speaker

Follow Author: @gof_general

Disclaimer:

The information in this ebook/book is provided for informational purposes only and should not be considered as professional advice. The author and publisher disclaim any responsibility for any adverse effects or consequences resulting from the use of the information herein.

Copyright © 2023 by Jon Green

All rights reserved. No part of this publication may be reproduced, distributed, or transmitted in any form or by any means, including photocopying, recording, or other electronic or mechanical methods, without the prior written permission of the publisher, except in the case of brief quotations embodied in critical reviews and certain other noncommercial uses permitted by copyright law.

Designed/Published by Jon Green

Made in United States
Orlando, FL
03 June 2024